THE HISTORY
OF MEXICO

AMY N. HUNTER

An ancient statue watches over the El Castillo pyramid in Yucatán. Mexico's history has seen the rise and fall of many unique civilizations.

OUR
SOUTHERN NEIGHBOR
MEXICO

THE HISTORY
OF MEXICO

AMY N. HUNTER

Mason Crest Publishers
Philadelphia

Mason Crest Publishers
370 Reed Road
Broomall PA 19008
www.masoncrest.com

First printing

1 3 5 7 9 8 6 4 2

Library of Congress Cataloging-in-Publication Data on file at the Library of Congress

ISBN 1-59084-079-8

TABLE OF CONTENTS

1. INDIAN SETTLEMENTS   11

2. THE SPANISH ARRIVE   19

3. INDEPENDENCE FOR MEXICO   27

4. THE UNREST CONTINUES   35

5. FINAL REVOLUTION   43

6. MODERN-DAY HOPES   49

   CHRONOLOGY   58

   GLOSSARY   60

   FURTHER READING   61

   INTERNET RESOURCES   62

   INDEX   63

OUR SOUTHERN NEIGHBOR MEXICO

THE ECONOMY OF MEXICO

FAMOUS PEOPLE OF MEXICO

THE FESTIVALS OF MEXICO

THE FOOD OF MEXICO

THE GEOGRAPHY OF MEXICO

THE GOVERNMENT OF MEXICO

THE HISTORY OF MEXICO

MEXICAN ART AND ARCHITECTURE

THE PEOPLE OF MEXICO

SPORTS OF MEXICO

THE GULF STATES OF MEXICO

THE STATES OF NORTHERN MEXICO

THE PACIFIC SOUTH STATES OF MEXICO

THE STATES OF CENTRAL MEXICO

THE PACIFIC NORTH STATES OF MEXICO

MEXICO: FACTS AND FIGURES

Roger E. Hernández
Senior Consulting Editor

INTRODUCTION

Mexico is a country in the midst of great change. And what happens in Mexico will have an important impact on the United States, its neighbor to the north.

These changes are being put in place by President Vicente Fox, who was elected in 2000. For the previous 71 years, power had been held by presidents from one single party, known in Spanish as *Partido Revolucionario Institucional* (Institutional Revolutionary Party, or PRI). Some of those presidents have been accused of corruption. President Fox, from a different party called *Partido de Acción Nacional* (National Action Party, or PAN), says he wants to eliminate that corruption. He also wants to have a friendlier relationship with the United States, and for American businesses to increase trade with Mexico. That will create more jobs, he says, and decrease poverty—which in turn will mean fewer Mexicans will find themselves forced to emigrate in search of a better life.

But it would be wrong to think of Mexico as nothing more than a poor country. Mexico has given the world some of its greatest artists and writers. Carlos Fuentes is considered one of the greatest living novelists, and poet-essayist Octavio Paz was awarded the Nobel Prize for Literature in 1990, the most prestigious honor a writer can win. Painters such as Diego Rivera and José Clemente Orozco specialized in murals, huge paintings done on walls that tell of the history of the nation. Another famous Mexican painter, Rufino Tamayo, blended the "cubist" style of modern European painters like Picasso with native folk themes.

Tamayo's paintings in many ways symbolize what Mexico is: A blend of the culture of Europe (more specifically, its Spanish version) and the indigenous cultures that predated the arrival of Columbus.

Those cultures were thriving even 3,000 years ago, when the Olmec people built imposing monuments that survive to this day in what are now the states of Tabasco and Veracruz. Later and further to the south in the Yucatán Peninsula, the Maya civilization flourished. They constructed cities in the midst of the jungle, complete with huge temples, courts in which ball games were played, and highly accurate calendars intricately carved in stone pillars. For some mysterious reason, the Mayans abandoned most of these great centers 1,100 years ago.

The Toltecs, in central Mexico, were the next major civilization. They were followed by the Aztecs. It was the Aztecs who built the city of Tenochitlán in the middle of a lake in what is now Mexico City, with long causeways connecting it to the mainland. By the early 1500s it was one of the largest cities anywhere, with perhaps 200,000 inhabitants.

Then the Spanish came. In 1519, twenty-seven years after Columbus arrived in the Americas, Hernán Cortés landed in Yucatán with just 600 soldiers plus a few cannons and horses. They marched inland, gaining allies as they went along among indigenous peoples who resented being ruled by the Aztecs. Within two years Cortés and the Spaniards ruled Mexico. They had conquered the Aztec Empire and devastated their great capital.

It was in that destruction that modern Mexico was born. The influence of the Aztecs and other indigenous people did not disappear even though untold numbers were killed. But neither can Mexico be recognized today without the Spanish influence.

Spain ruled for three centuries. Then in 1810 Mexicans began a struggle for independence from colonial Spain, much like the United States had fought for its own independence from Great Britain. In 1821 Mexico finally became an independent nation.

The newly born republic faced many difficulties. There was much poverty, especially among descendants of indigenous peoples; most of the wealth and political power was in the hands of a small elite of Spanish ancestry. To make things worse, Mexico lost almost half of its territory to the United States in a war that lasted from 1846 to 1848. Many still resent the loss of territory, which accounts for lingering anti-American sentiments among some Mexicans. The country was later occupied by France, but under national hero Benito Juárez Mexico regained its independence in 1867.

The next turning point in Mexican history came in 1911, when a revolution meant to help the millions of Mexicans stuck in poverty began against dictator Porfirio Díaz. There was violence and fighting until 1929, when Plutarco Elías Calles founded what was to become the *Partido Revolucionario Institucional*. It brought stability as well as economic progress. Yet millions of Mexicans remained in poverty, and as time went on PRI rulers became increasingly corrupt.

It was the desire of the people of Mexico to trust someone other than the candidate of PRI that resulted in the election of Fox. And so this nation of more than 100 million, with its ancient heritage, its diverse mestizo culture, its grinding poverty, and its glorious arts, stands on the brink of a new era. Modern Mexico is seeking a place as the leader of all Latin America, an ally of the United States, and an important voice in global politics. For that to happen, Mexico must narrow the gap between the rich and poor and bring more people in the middle class. It will be interesting to watch as Fox and the Mexican people work to bring their country into the first rank of nations.

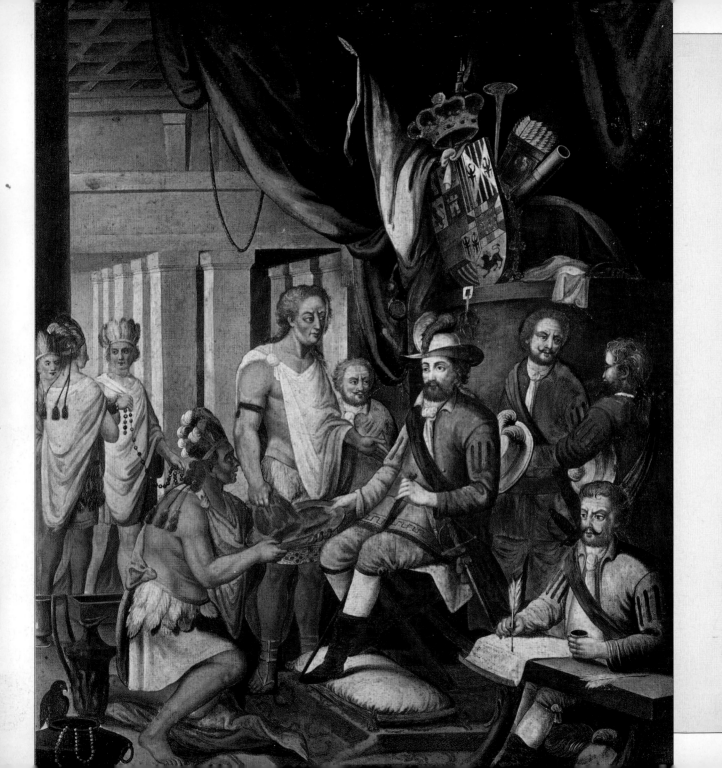

INDIAN SETTLEMENTS

The first civilization to inhabit Mexico was probably the Olmecs. Historians believe that the Olmecs may have arrived in Mexico as early as 2000 B.C. They were once thought to have settled in the Southern Coastal Plains, but the discovery of new ruins suggests that they may have originally settled on the Pacific Coast.

The Olmec civilization is perhaps best known for making the "Olmec Heads." These were sculptures made of stone. They combined the features of humans and jaguars, and wore helmets. These sculptures were set on important sites, and are lasting reminders of this ancient culture.

The Olmecs are credited with developing a system of numbering, a calendar, and writing. They are believed to be the first people in the

In this 17th century painting, the Aztec emperor Montezuma II bows in respect to Hernán Cortes. The surprising victory of a handful of Spanish conquistadors over the vast Aztec empire helped to shape Mexico's history for several hundred years.

New World to develop religious centers and pyramids. These accomplishments earned them the title "mother culture" for the generations of Indian civilizations that followed. Despite all of the advances made by the Olmec culture, however, by 400 B.C., the Olmec tribe had disappeared completely, probably overrun by warriors from other areas. Eventually the other Indian settlements, such as the Zapotec and the Mixtee, were abandoned as well.

But the culture of all these long-ago tribes still plays an important role in Mexico, for it continues to influence the art and culture of today's Mexicans. Mexican artists draw inspiration from these ancient roots, and the food, the language, and even the games that Mexicans enjoy all contain echoes from these long-ago ancestors.

The city of Teotihuacán was one of the earliest and largest cities to develop in Mexico. Located in the Valley of Mexico, it was a cultural and economic center. Eight miles square, the city was filled with large pyramids, wide streets, and a variety of shops and religious centers. There even appear to have been apartment complexes. At its peak, 125,000 people lived in Teotihuacán, civilized people who developed writing and books, as well as a numbering

The Olmecs are thought to be the original inventors of the game *tlachtli* (although later cultures like the Aztecs also played this game). The game is played on a court shaped like a capital H. Two sides compete, attempting to knock the ball into the opponent's side of the court. Although the contestants wore heavy padding, serious injury and even death resulted in some of these competitions. Nevertheless it was considered an exciting sport for nobles to watch and usually a good deal of betting took place on the outcome of the game.

This giant Olmec head was brought from its original setting, the ruins of La Venta, to the Tabascan capital. The poet Carlos Pellecer designed this site for the artifact.

system. Teotihuacán began to decline around A.D. 650 and was abandoned entirely by A.D. 750. There are a variety of theories about the fall of Teotihuacán, but we will probably never know for sure what took place to end this civilization. Whatever happened completely destroyed all records that may have been kept. The cause of the fall of Teotihuacán will likely remain a mystery.

But other new cultures arose in Mexico. The Maya were the most influential culture in early Mexico. During the peak of their power, their empire stretched throughout the Mexican states of Chiapas, Tabasco, Campeche, Yucatán, and Quintana. They even extended into what are now the countries of Guatemala, Belize, and Honduras. The influence of the Teotihuacán culture on Mayan culture is apparent. Both groups wore similar clothing, their art and religious symbols were similar, and both built tall, stepped pyramids. Historians believe that a combination of war, famine, and disease may have combined to cause the fall of both Teotihuacán and, years later, the Mayan civilization.

From A.D. 900 to the arrival of the Spanish early in the 16th century, war was a constant feature of Mexican culture. While priests and other religious

This mural depicting Aztec life is displayed in the Palacio Nacional in Mexico City. The Aztecs built a powerful civilization during the 15th century. Today, however, few of their customs are reflected in Mexican life.

The legend of the Aztecs says that the god of war led them south from their original home. Where they saw an eagle perched on a cactus with a snake in its beak, they were to build their new capital. This is where they constructed their city of Tenochtitlán, which is also the site of modern-day Mexico City.

15

The capital of Mexico was not always known as Mexico City. This painting shows the city as it appeared in the 16th century, when it was known as Tenochtitlán.

leaders had ruled earlier cultures, military kings began to take control of the various groups of Indians. The different groups struggled among themselves for control of the land and people.

The Toltecs were the first group to gain significant victories. Between A.D. 900 and 1200, the Toltecs controlled land from Hidalgo north to Zacatecas, south to Guatemala, and east to the pyramids of Chichen Itza. An uneasy peace existed between the Zapotecs and Mixtes of Oaxaca, the

The Aztecs were a powerful civilization in their time, and they worshipped their rulers as gods. This portrait of Montezuma II, the last Aztec king, shows him dressed in clothes inlaid with jewels.

Tarascans of Michoacan, and the Huastecs of northeast Mexico. This would change with the arrival of the Aztecs from the north.

The Aztecs arrived in Mexico as savages, but they quickly learned the customs of the other Indian civilizations. The Aztecs were soon improving on the methods of agriculture and building developed by th Maya and Toltecs.

In 1325 the Aztecs began to build Tenochtitlán, their new capital. The Aztecs formed an alliance with the Tepanec people. First, the Aztec served as the Tepanecs' warriors, but eventually, by 1428, the Aztecs overthrew the Tepanecs and seized control of the Valley of Mexico.

By 1500, the Aztecs controlled all the lands and people of central Mexico. Aztec warriors believed that they were destined to die in battle. According to their beliefs, upon their death they would becom hummingbirds and fly to the sun. This lack of fear while doing battle helped them to achieve rapid and total control of central Mexico. The tribes the Aztecs conquered had to pay tribute and taxes in the form of precious stones, metals, feathers, and food.

By the arrival of the Spanish *conquistadors* in 1519, the Aztecs were the most dominant force in Middle America. Nahuatl, the langua of the Aztecs, was spoken from Panama to western North America. Nahuatl is still spoken by Indians in several parts of Mexico today.

THE SPANISH ARRIVE

In the 15th century, Spain was the most powerful country in Europe. The Spaniards' strong Roman Catholic beliefs taught them that their god was to rule the world. This led to their desire to explore new areas. In 1492, Christopher Columbus landed in the Caribbean, and the Catholic pope granted Spain ownership of all the lands in this New World, as long as they made the name of God known there. The Spaniards quickly established a colony in Cuba, naming Diego Velazquez as governor. Velazquez sent Francisco Hernandez de Cordoba and Juan de Grivalva on for further exploration. They returned to Cuba with reports of massive wealth and population along the Yucatán peninsula. Velazquez then sent Hernán Cortés to investigate further.

Cortés was given 11 small ships, 110 sailors, 553 soldiers, and 16 horses to aid him on his expedition. Representatives of Montezuma, the Aztec king, greeted the Spaniards as soon as they landed. Believing the Spaniards to be gods, the Aztecs immediately provided Cortés and his men with gold and other valuables as gifts. Cortés, convinced that this was a chance to win glory in Spain, decided to conquer this new land. Afraid that his men might abandon him, he burned his ships as a way to communicate that there was no going back. They were in this new land to stay.

Cortés established the city of Veracruz on the coast of Mexico and appointed one of his soldiers as governor. This governor then granted Cortés permission to conquer the New World and claim it as Spain's.

Despite the fact that the Aztec kingdom consisted of over 5 million people and dozens of city-states in addition to the capital at Tenochtitlán, Cortes had several advantages. The Aztecs believed that the Spaniards were gods, and that their arrival had been predicted in religious stories. The Spaniards were also armed with **crossbows**, armor, cannons, and swords. Perhaps the Cortes' greatest **asset** was the smoldering hatred that many other native groups felt for the Aztec rulers.

Forced to pay huge tribute to Tenochtitlán for many years, many of the Indian tribes were eager to help Cortés and his men overtake the Aztecs. One tribe that lived on the Gulf Coast provided Cortés with Doña Marina, a young Indian woman who acted as translator and advisor to Cortés. With her help, Cortés was able to determine the

Friar Bartolome de las Casas arrived in New Spain in 1531. He recognized that the Spaniards were not treating the Indians fairly and worked tirelessly to defend them. In his position as a king-appointed missionary, he wrote a book condemning the Spaniards' treatment of the Indians; the book was published and read in Europe. He worked for the fair and equal treatment of Indians until his death in 1566. Although his work did not directly provide equal treatment of the Indians, it opened the eyes of many Europeans to the atrocities happening in the New World.

weaknesses of the Aztecs, as well as convince many Indians to join the side of the Spaniards.

Cortés's first strategy for doing battle with the Aztecs was to approach Tenochtitlán along the narrow causeway that extended through the lake on which the city was built. Montezuma, expecting Cortés and his men to be friendly, readily invited them into the fortress. The Spaniards captured Montezuma, and a bloody battle ensued. Angry that their king had betrayed them to the white men, Montezuma's own men killed him in the confusion, but Cortés and the Spaniards were forced to retreat. Many Spaniards were killed, and Cortés knew he must formulate a new plan.

He realized that he would not be able to use the narrow strip of land to

Hernán Cortés perhaps did more than anyone to change Mexican life. Cortés was able to conquer the powerful Aztecs so easily in part because they may have believed he was a god.

22

The Spaniards were disgusted by the religious rituals of the Aztecs, especially those involving human sacrifice. They banned these practices and forced many native Mexicans to convert to Christianity.

approach Tenochtitlán again. He decided to gather all the sails and *rigging* from the remains of the ships the Spaniards had arrived on, and sent his men to cut lumber in the forests. Reinforcements of supplies and horses arrived from Cuba while Cortés was making his preparations. With the help of over 8,000 friendly Indians, these materials were carried over the mountains to the shore of the lake surrounding Tenochtitlán. Cortés then began the construction of a small *armada*, with the idea of waging a water attack on the unsuspecting Aztecs. By April 1521, Cortés had assembled 13 warships with cannons, a fleet of canoes with armed Indians, over 900 armed Spanish soldiers, including 84 horsemen, and thousands of Indian warriors on foot.

But the biggest asset that Cortés had was *smallpox* and other diseases. Before the arrival of the Spaniards, the natives had never been exposed to these illnesses. They soon became sick, and that, combined with the Spaniards cutting off their food and water supply, caused a serious situation for the Indians. Once Cuauhtemoc, the new Aztec king, was captured, the Aztec capital soon fell. On August 13, 1521, barely 90 days into the battle, the Spaniards conquered Tenochtitlán.

The Spaniards established a new city on the ruins of Tenochtitlán, and began calling the surrounding land New Spain. Cortés sent his men out to explore New Spain and conquer the remaining Indian tribes.

Quetzalcoatl was considered the wisest and most kind of the Aztec gods. In most drawings he was depicted as having a beard. According to Aztec legend, Quetzalcoatl was forced out of his land by another god. He promised that he would return in the year that the Europeans numbered as 1519. During that year, a messenger arrived in Tenochtitlán and told Montezuma of strange men with light skin and facial hair. Their appearance on the shore of Mexico, seemingly from nowhere, along with the horses they brought, which the Aztecs had never seen, convinced Montezuma of one thing: Quetzalcoatl had returned. Based on this assumption, Montezuma and his men accommodated Cortés and his men, offering gifts and inviting them into their fortress. This was a deadly mistake. With such an advantage, it is no wonder that Cortés was able to defeat the Aztecs so easily.

23

Mexico City was not the only important ancient site in Mexico. Veracruz boasts its own ruins, among them the Temple of Chimneys. Building temples and pyramids to the gods was an important part of ancient Mexican society.

Cortés and his men believed that the Aztecs were preparing to stage a revolt, with Cuauhtemoc's encouragement. In 1524, Cuauhtemoc, who was still being held as a prisoner of the Spaniards, was executed. With the Aztecs totally defeated, by 1525 New Spain had expanded southward to present day Guatemala and Honduras. The Mayan Indians proved to be the most difficult for the Spanish to conquer. They retained control of the Yucatán peninsula for another 20 years or more and remained independent in some areas of Mexico for over 150 years.

The Spaniards spent a great deal of time expanding their settlements to the north, where rich deposits of gold and silver were located. Franciscan and Jesuit priests were among the first permanent settlers in the area. Through the development of mission fortresses, the priests worked to convert the Indians to the Catholic faith and discourage them from raiding the silver and gold mines that the Spaniards constructed. When the Spaniards could not convert the Indians to their faith willingly, they resorted to military force. Relationships with the Indians were strained, largely due to the Spaniards' enslavement of them. In 1537 the Catholic pope officially discouraged slavery, but ill will remained.

With no immunity to the diseases that the Spanish brought with them, Native Americans died in great numbers. The poor treatment that they received as slaves to their Spanish master also caused many deaths. From 1519 to 1700, the population of Indians dropped from over 25 million to around 1 million.

While the Aztecs and other ancient civilizations of Mexico worshipped their own gods, Spanish rulers believed it was their responsibility to spread Christianity to as many souls as possible. In order to achieve this, they built missions to house the padres who preached to the natives.

INDEPENDENCE FOR MEXICO

By 1600, Spain controlled most of what is now Mexico. Governing this vast area was proving to be very difficult, however. The distance from Europe as well as the unhappiness of the general population led to many problems.

Missionaries established most of the governments of New Spain. In the 16th century, these missionaries built, with the help of Indians who had converted to Christianity, over 100,000 churches and convents. The churches acted as local governments in most areas of New Spain. By three centuries later, the Catholic Church owned over half of the buildings in Mexico. Church property was not taxed, so Spain did not enjoy the wealth that was developing in New Spain at this time.

New Spain also spent a great deal of time and effort developing its silver mines. During this period of **colonialism**, the world's production of silver doubled, thanks to **exports** from New Spain. The Spanish settlers also developed *haciendas*, or large ranches. The wealth of New

Spain rested mainly with a small group of *criollos* that owned these haciendas and silver mines. Criollos were pureblooded Spaniards who were born in New Spain.

But Spanish law prevented criollos from holding political office. At the time only *gachupines*, or Spaniards actually born in Spain, were permitted to become officials. This caused much resentment among the criollos. Growing populations of Spanish-Indians, known as *mestizos*, were also becoming impatient with the Spaniards' treatment of Indians.

While the American and French Revolutions were being fought, many settlers of New Spain began to question the government. The world was full of new ideas about government and **democracy**, and people in New Spain began to take a fresh look at how they wanted to live. Anger at the oppression of the Indians combined with the criollos' desire for free trade with countries other than Spain; the combination caused a number of unlikely allies. As a result, many of the priests gathered criollos on their side and declared their desire for independence from Spain.

In 1804, King Charles III of Spain ordered that all church funds should be given to Spain. Since the churches had acted as banks for the criollos, this caused

Jose Maria Morelos, a priest who strongly agreed with the revolution, took up the challenge of leadership after Hidalgo was executed. Morelos had spent the early years of his priesthood working with mestizos and Indians. He joined with Hidalgo in 1811, and after Hidalgo's death he fought tirelessly for the revolution. In 1813 he drafted the Congress of Chilpancingo. This document was the basis for a constitution. In November of the same year, the rebels declared independence from Spain. Spanish forces soon caught up with Morelos and his men, and Morelos was shot as a traitor.

The policies of Spanish king Charles III, who is shown in this painting by Francisco Jose de Goya y Lucientes, caused many problems for the people of Mexico, or New Spain, as it was known at that time. When he financially drained the churches of New Spain, Mexico was ready to fight for independence.

Napoleon Bonaparte's plans to conquer Europe inadvertantly helped the Mexican cause for independence. His 1808 invasion weakened Spain's government, which gave the Mexican people an opportunity to throw off the oppressive Spanish rule.

tremendous problems for many of the people of New Spain.

The plans for revolution might have fallen apart, however, if not for Napoleon Bonaparte. Bonaparte had taken control of France, and when he sought to extend his power into Spain in 1808, his invasion caused the Spanish king a great deal of hardship. Struggling to retain control of Spain, the Spanish government had few resources left to deal with New Spain. The conditions were ripe for revolution.

On September 16, 1810, a priest from the city of Delores issued a proclamation calling for the end of Spanish rule. Miguel Hidalgo y Costilla had long been troubled by the oppression of Native Americans. He was a friend of the Indians, teaching them farming methods and pottery. Under Spanish rule, this was illegal, and the viceroy of New Spain planned to arrest him. In response, Hidalgo issued his *Grito de Delores* (Cry of Delores), calling for self-rule, equality among the different groups living in New Spain, and redistribution of land from the wealthy to the ~~poor~~. This marked the beginning of the revolt.

A leader of the criollos who was planning to overthrow the gachupines was Ignacio Allende. Allende, a former officer in the Spanish army, was a main force in the criollos' fight for freedom. When he heard that Hidalgo was to be arrested, he joined forces with the priest. The two men hoped to avoid a battle with Spain by convincing the army to support them rather than the gachupines. The men gathered supporters of criollos, mestizos, and Indians, and moved into Mexico City.

Despite the leaders' peaceful intentions, the years of mistreatment at the hands of the Spaniards had taken their toll. Once the rebellion had the govern-

Napoleon Bonaparte was a French general whose main goal was the expansion of France through the conquest of Europe. King Charles the IV of Spain fell into disfavor with the Spanish people by allowing Bonaparte to occupy Lisbon. As King Charles the IV prepared to abdicate the throne to his son, Ferdinand VII, Napoleon decided that he should end Spanish rule entirely. He forced King Charles and Ferdinand to abdicate, and appointed Joseph Bonaparte to rule Spain. The Spanish people disliked this, and through a violent upheaval, they drove Napoleon and his men out of Spain and Portugal. This was the beginning of the end of Napoleon's conquest of Europe.

Jose Maria Morelos was a revolutionary Catholic priest who received the title of Generalissimo of the Mexican Army. Though he was executed by the Spanish, his determination was revered and exemplified by the Mexican people.

ment in its sight, a bloody battle ensued. Despite early victory, the viceroy managed to squash the rebellion in 1811. Hidalgo and Allende were executed, but new leaders emerged from this battle, and *civil* war and revolution would continue for 75 more years. ✳ *Read this here!*

The continual battles took their toll on the governments and people of New Spain. Soon the gachupine leaders began to desire freedom from Spain as well. Their desire for freedom was more self-serving, however, since they actually hoped to gain more wealth and power by becoming independent. They united secretly with the revolutionaries and drafted the *Plan de Iguala*. The plan declared Mexico an independent nation. Its inhabitants were to be equal, whether they were from European or native descent. Spain, thousands of miles away, did not see any way to refuse the proposition, and the plan was signed in 1821. One provision that Spain made was that a representative from the Spanish government head the new government in Mexico City. By the time this representative arrived from Spain, however, the new Mexican government had united and forced him to sign the Treaty of Cordoba. This treaty, signed by the king's representative, Juan O'Donoju, on August 24, 1821, ended Spain's involvement in New Spain.

✳ Among the many heroes of the uprising are women. Josefa put the revolution in motion by warning Hidalgo the Spanish had uncovered their plot.

33

In this colored Mexican illustration, Agustin de Iturbide rides triumphantly into Mexico City in 1821. Iturbide, a Mexican military leader, became emperor of Mexico but his government soon fell during a revolt. He was exiled in 1823; when he returned a year later, Iturbude was captured and executed.

THE UNREST CONTINUES

Mexico's independence from Spain was only the beginning of a violent period of internal and external struggle. One group in Mexico wanted the nation to be ruled as a *republic*, while another group wanted it ruled as an *empire*. Initially the group that wanted an empire won, and Agustin de Iturbide was appointed king. He lasted only two years before being overthrown.

The new government established Mexico as a republic, the United States of Mexico. They drafted a new *constitution* in 1824, dividing the country into 19 states, four territories, and a federal district. The constitution also called for an end to slavery and granted all men the right to vote. Although a step in the right direction, severe restrictions in the laws made it impossible for the poorest citizens to vote. Unrest continued. The government, unstable from fighting and without many of the Spaniards who had grown wealthy in the mines and haciendas, was nearly broke. When the government could not pay the military's wages, the military seized control and created a new government.

This new government borrowed money from other countries to keep itself afloat. Instead of using the money to develop the country's resources, the money was spent to pay off the government's debt. As soon as that money was gone, another revolt occurred.

Antonio López de Santa Anna, an army general, was initially charged with ridding the country of Spaniards. As his ambition grew, he began seizing power. In 1824, he revoked the constitution. He appointed himself president and was in and out of office 11 times between 1833 and 1855.

As Americans began settling in northern Mexico, they talked of establishing their own country, independent of Mexico. By 1834, the Americans outnumbered the Mexicans in the northern part of Mexico. In 1835, these settlers declared their independence. Santa Anna attacked the Americans at the Alamo, defeating them soundly. At a later battle in San Jacinto, however, the Americans defeated the Mexicans and captured Santa Anna. Santa Anna was forced to sign the Velasco Agreement in 1836, giving northern Mexico its freedom.

Mexico, furious over this loss, *exiled* Santa Anna and refused to recognize the Velasco Agreement. For nine years, this area in northern Mexico was in limbo. It considered itself a free state, but Mexico still considered it part of the country. Finally, the United States admitted the land into the Union, and it became the state of Texas.

This caused Mexico to declare war on the United States. The Mexican government reconciled with Santa Anna, and asked him to lead the war against the United States. The United States troops were led by General Zachary Taylor, and they were much better prepared for battle than the Mexican troops. American forces captured Mexico City on September 14, 1847; the Mexican-American war was officially over on February 2, 1848, when the Treaty of Guadalupe Hidalgo was signed. This treaty called for Mexico to turn over all land north of the Río Grande River (Texas), as well as all the land from the Gila River to the Pacific Ocean (what is now California, Nevada, Utah, and Arizona, as well as parts of Wyoming, Colorado, and New Mexico).

Despite Santa Anna's military failures, Mexico allowed him to name himself dictator of Mexico. In order to raise funds for the military, he sold additional land to the United States. In 1854 he sold a piece of Mexico along the Gila River (present-day Arizona and New Mexico) to the United States for 10 million dollars. This deal, called the Gadsden Purchase, was the last major change of Mexican boundary lines. Mexico had lost over 50 percent of its territory to the United States in just a few short years.

Santa Anna was removed from power for the final time in 1855.

Agustin de Iturbide was the first leader of Mexico once it won its independence. Responsible for the *Plan de Iguala*, which declared independence from Spain, guaranteed equality among the races, and stated that the Catholic Church would be the official church of Mexico, Iturbide was considered a military hero. Once he appointed himself ruler of Mexico, however, many of the people began to feel that rule by Iturbide would not be any better than rule by Spain. The Mexican people wanted their independence, and within two years Santa Anna had overthrown Iturbide. Iturbide abdicated the throne and moved to Europe. The next year he returned to Mexico, unaware that the government had called for his death. On July 19, 1824, Iturbide was executed. The Catholic Church still considers Iturbide a hero for the emphasis that he placed on the importance of the Catholic religion.

38

Antonio López de Santa Anna was a Mexican soldier, president, and dictator. Though he was a respected military man, his troops suffered a sound defeat at the battle of San Jacinto. This misstep led to the loss of a large chunk of northern Mexico, which later became part of the United States as the state of Texas.

Benito Juárez was appointed minister of justice and began a process of reform and rebuilding. Juárez was a strong believer in the anticlerical movement, which sought to make the Catholic Church less important to the economy. A new constitution was drafted in 1857, but three years of battles passed before Juárez and his men were able to capture and maintain control of Mexico City. Juárez was named president of Mexico and began efforts to rebuild the nation's economy.

During this rebuilding stage, Mexico quit making payments on loans from England, Spain, and France. Although Juárez tried to assure the countries that this was only a temporary situation until the economy of Mexico was stabilized, the countries, on the advice of the conservative government that Juárez had overthrown, sent warships to Mexico.

While England and Spain only wanted their money, France, ruled at the time by Napoleon III, nephew of Napoleon Bonaparte, thought this would be an opportunity to expand France's power into the New World.

Benito Pablo Juárez was born to Zapotec Indian parents in Oaxaca. He went on to twice be elected president of his country. His main goal was to apply some degree of reform to the tumultuous government of Mexico.

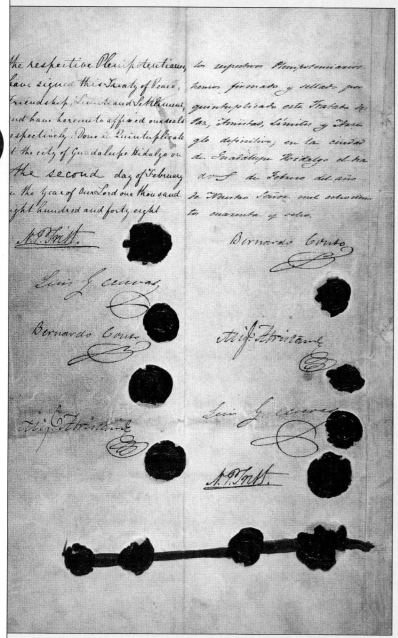

England and Spain quickly withdrew their troops, but France invaded Mexico on May 5, 1862. Initially, Mexico was able to hold off the assault, but on June 10, 1863, Mexico City was captured. Juárez was forced to go into hiding in northern Mexico.

In 1864, Napoleon appointed Maximilian, archduke of Austria, as the emperor of Mexico.

The Treaty of Guadalupe Hidalgo ended the Mexican War, at a vast sacrifice of Mexican land. The United States gained 1,193,061 square miles to its territory through this agreement, including New Mexico and California.

Unwelcome by the Mexicans, Maximilian had a difficult time establishing an effective government in Mexico. Finally, after the American Civil War ended, the United States became interested in driving France out of Mexico. Between the pressure applied by the United States and problems in France, including the threat of an invasion by Prussia, Napoleon soon withdrew his troops from Mexico and returned to France.

But Maximilian refused to return to Europe when Napoleon withdrew his troops. He had worked hard for the interests of the Mexican people, and now he believed they wanted him to remain as leader. His wife, Carlota, traveled to Europe, seeking support for her husband. She went insane, however, and her husband was captured and executed by the Mexican troops soon after.

Juárez was reelected as president of Mexico, and he set about trying to strengthen the economy of Mexico. He created *infrastructure*, such as railroads and schools, and reduced the size of the military, which cost a considerable amount of money to operate.

In 1872, some army officials, led by a general by the name of Porfirio Díaz, attempted a *coup* on Juárez's government. This failed attempt was a sign of the unrest that was to come. Juárez died of a heart attack in 1873 and was succeeded by Sebastian Lerdo. Lerdo's reelection attempt in 1876 failed, and Porfirio Díaz became president of Mexico.

Mexican revolutionaries Pancho Villa (left) and Emiliano Zapata (right) sit in the middle of this photograph, taken in 1915. Villa and Zapata are flanked by two fellow revolutionaries, Tomás Urbina and Otilio Montaño.

FINAL REVOLUTION

Díaz was a ruthless dictator. Although relatively uneducated, he cared little for the plight of the poorer people of Mexico, and his rule was marked by the increased wealth of Mexico's upper class. He did not accept any questioning of his authority, and his government worked quickly to squash any protest by the Mexican citizens. Díaz created a police force known as the *Rurales*. The *Rurales* were given extreme latitude in what they were allowed to do, and they frequently used violence to maintain order.

Most of Díaz's rule resulted in no economic improvements for Mexico, but during his last 16 years in office, Díaz brought Jose Ives Limantour to Mexico to develop the economy. Limantour surrounded himself with well-educated men and worked tirelessly to build the treasury of Mexico. Foreign companies began to mine the nation's silver and gold and develop the oil deposits. By the end of Díaz's rule, foreign trade had increased 10 times from what it had been under Juárez's presidency.

From the outside, it appeared that Mexico was on a successful track, both economically and politically. Internally, things were not going so well. Wealthy landowners had acquired most of the land in Mexico, and the majority of the citizens worked for these landowners as little more than slaves. They were forced to go into debt to the landowners; due to poor wages and unfair labor practices, they were then never able to rid themselves of the debt. The debt would even pass from one generation to the next.

In the cities, small political groups were emerging that were growing tired of Díaz's oppressive rule. This movement, known as *Regeneración* (Regeneration), staged **strikes** and peaceful protests. They resented the oppression caused by Díaz and wanted freedom for themselves and their fellow citizens. Díaz ruthlessly stopped these protests with deadly battles.

In 1910, Francisco Madero ran for president against Díaz. Díaz had Madero arrested and claimed victory in the election. When Madero was released from prison, he moved to the United States. From there, he began to plan a way to conquer Díaz. On November 20, 1910, Madero declared that the election was void and stated that the people of Mexico should stand up for their rights. Various small rebellions sprung up across Mexico.

44

Alvaro Obregon is credited with restoring order to the chaos that was rampant in Mexico during and after the Revolution. Not only was Obregon able to maintain peace during this difficult time, but he also improved the Mexican school system. A long-term problem for the citizens of Mexico had been that the government largely ignored them. Obregon, with his priorities on peace and education, was popular with the people. He was less popular with the United States, who considered him radical because of his desire to reclaim Mexico's oil reserves. Shortly after his reelection he was assassinated by Jose de Leon Torro, who considered him responsible for the persecution of Christians.

Díaz managed to resist most of these threats, but in the state of Chihuahua, a small group, led by Pancho Villa, managed to fend off Díaz's men. Madero joined forces with Villa and Pascual Orozco, and together they made a serious effort to gain control of Mexico. Díaz, elderly and aware that he was losing power, resigned as president and moved to Paris.

Madero was elected president and immediately sought to prove his leadership. When Emiliano Zapata, a key figure in helping Madero drive Díaz from Mexico, asked Madero to return land that had been seized by Díaz, he refused. Zapata, Pancho Villa, and other former supporters now began to wage war against Madero and his government. Madero was arrested and shot by the group, and General Victoriano Huerta, who betrayed Madero and was responsible for his arrest, was named president. Huerta also did not want to return the seized land, and Zapata and Villa continued their *guerrilla* tactics.

Francisco Indalecio Madero was a Mexican revolutionary and politician. He opposed President Diaz and overtook the presidency for two years, at which point his reign was overthown.

45

Ejidos are lands that are jointly owned by a group of citizens. Initially, this was the process that the Indians used, but even today over 55 percent of the property of Mexico is owned in this way. The ejidos typically consist of farmland, pastures, and a small township. The land is owned communally, but each family has a section that they can work independently. This process works well, for most citizens cannot afford large areas of land privately; owned jointly and passed through generations of families, it is an affordable way to live.

The revolution might have lasted indefinitely had it not been for the intervention of the United States. Woodrow Wilson had been elected president of the United States, and he strongly supported the Mexican Revolution's efforts. He allowed the shipment of guns and ammunition to the rebels and sent troops to occupy Veracruz. With the United States on the side of the rebels, Huerta fled the country.

A battle for power ensued between Pancho Villa and Alvaro Obregon. Eventually many of Villa's men were killed in battle with Plutarco Elias Calles. With Villa losing such an important battle, the United States withdrew its support and Venustiano Carranza was named president.

Alvaro Obregon was elected twice to the Mexican presidency. His most notable accomplishment was helping to restore order to the country after its destructive civil war.

On February 5, 1917, Mexico adopted a new constitution, under the guidance of Carranza, and it is still used today. The new constitution reduced the power of the church and discouraged the hacienda system that had caused such inequality throughout Mexico. Although the new constitution stated that the government would provide for social and economic development of the people, in reality Carranza never fully adopted these proposals.

In 1920, he was assassinated while trying to flee the country. With Carranza gone, Obregon became president. His presidency, beginning in 1921, marked the end of the long period of unrest and the beginning of reform in modern-day Mexico.

Venustiano Carranza, a leader of moderate forces in the Mexican Revolution, became the first president of the Mexican Republic. Under his rule, the Mexican government created a constitution that still applies today.

A native woman tries to avoid teargas fired on her by Mexican riot police. She is a supporter of the Zapatista National Liberation Army (EZLN), taking part in a movement to keep Mexican authorities from increasing their presence in the troubled Mexican state of Chiapas.

MODERN-DAY HOPES

Obregon's presidency lasted for four years, and his work to rebuild Mexico was appreciated by the people. Plutarco Elias Calles, who supported the constitution and ideals of Mexico, *succeeded* him. Unfortunately, the longer Calles was in power, the more dictatorial he became. Church uprisings and mediation on the part of the United States caused Calles to back off on some of his ideas, including his plan to usher Obregon back into office at the end of Calles' term. Instead, Lazaro Cardenas was appointed president, with the support of Calles, and began to strengthen the labor movement within Mexico. Calles disagreed with this tactic, but Cardenas was a popular leader, and Calles was forced into exile.

Cardenas developed the Mexican election system that is still in use today. He also masterminded the move that allowed Mexico to develop its economic independence. For many years foreign countries had developed the oil in Mexico, with Mexico not receiving any of the profits. In 1938, Cardenas nationalized the oil industry and seized the foreign company's holdings. Britain was angered by the move, and the United States nearly considered declaring war on Mexico. Instead, due to

Vicente Fox, elected president on December 1, 2000, is a member of the National Action Party, the first party other than the PRI to hold power in over 70 years. Fox is a graduate of Harvard University in the United States, and he worked for Coca-Cola before entering politics. He is expected to concentrate on the development of small business and diversifying the government. Fox can also be expected to work toward additional reforms within the election process, as well as strengthening the judicial system, which has been a long time weakness in Mexico. Most Mexicans are excited about the chance for the first real change in decades.

negotiations between Cardenas and President Franklin D. Roosevelt, Mexico agreed to pay for the land but retain the oil rights. It took Mexico until 1962 to repay the debt of over 100 million dollars, but once they did, they were able to profit from the oil and develop their economic freedom. The growth of the oil trade, as well as natural gas production and the development of factories led to growth in the middle class of Mexico.

Mexico helped the United States immensely during World War II, both in production of materials and sending troops into battle, and this helped to develop a strong relationship between America and Mexico that continues to this day. Along with this close relationship came the realization by the Mexican people of what a truly free society was like. The Mexican people could look to the United States as a role model. What they saw, however, made them less happy with their own government, and again tension began to build.

In 1968, Mexico was slated to host the Olympic Games. This was a considerable honor, and the Mexican government took it very seriously. But on the eve of the opening ceremonies, thousands of students began protesting the political system. President Gustavo Díaz Ordaz ordered federal troops to fire on the students. Hundreds of students were killed in the demonstrations, and the international news services were a witness to this violent act. This was the beginning of worldwide pressure for Mexico to clean up its act.

A serious of important and damaging blunders by the government added strength to the citizens' desire for reform. Loans that the government had taken out in the 1970s nearly crippled the Mexican

52

economy in the early '80s when the price of oil dropped substantially. Mexico was unable to meet even the minimum payment on its debt, and many foreign companies became nervous about investing in Mexico. An earthquake in 1985 caused mass destruction to parts of Mexico, and again the government was inadequate in its response. The slow response time and insufficient aid was typical of what the citizens had come to expect from the government. The final straw came in 1988 when the suspicion of massive vote fraud propelled many to denounce the entire political system.

Plutarco Elias Calles was president during a time of struggle between church and state in Mexico. Though popular at the beginning of his term, after he stepped down as president Calles was eventually forced into exile.

The Zapatista National Liberation Army (EZLN) is a guerilla group that has organized armed resistance against the Mexican government. This photo of a Zapatista was taken in 1995 in the Chiapas province of Mexico.

In 1989, the Partido de la Revolution Democratica (PRD) was formed as a counterpart to the existing *conservative* political party (PRI). But by 1994 the economy of Mexico was collapsing. The value of the *peso* had dropped, while the prices of products were rising. Despite this downturn in the economy and the people's general distrust, Ernesto Zedillo, a candidate for the conservative PRI, was elected in 1994. The general thinking was that the election was *rigged*, and the people's discontent grew.

Between 1989 and 1997 over 400 members of the *liberal* PRD were kidnapped, tortured, or murdered. The main difference between the corruption and violence that riddled Mexico now and the problems that it had faced earlier in its history was that now the reports of violence were broadcast on a world stage. The advent of radio, television, and news wire services meant that Mexico's problems were known to the entire world. If Mexico hoped to develop its economy, it would have to improve the treatment of its citizens. By 1997, the Mexican people had had enough. The PRI lost its congressional majority, several governorships, and the position of mayor in Mexico City.

Progress to improve the life of Mexico's citizens has been slow, but there has been progress. Mexico still has its troubles. For instance, Mexican children receive an average of only five years of school. The rapid growth in population that Mexico has experienced has also led to problems. While struggling to develop its natural and

One interesting development that has occurred as Mexican political groups have struggled to organize is the alliances that have formed. For example, Hellmuth Schleiter formed the political party Union Nacional Sinarquista in 1947. Schleiter was a German, teaching college in Mexico. Although no one knew it at the time, he was also a German intelligence agent. His organization stood for strength of the Catholic Church, and it opposed liberalism and the United States. At its peak the group had over a million members and was a strong supporter of the fascism being practiced by Hitler and Mussolini. Over time this organization has become more moderate and evolved into the political party responsible for many of the social and political changes that have occurred in Mexico.

economic resources, Mexico has at the same time experienced a population growth that has made it impossible to expand services and schooling to all citizens. This rapid population growth has also led to difficulties in access to health care. Although the government of Mexico plans to eventually offer medical care to everyone, at this point many basic health services are difficult to obtain.

Violence continues to remain a part of Mexico's culture. The organization of the Zapatista National Liberation Army (EZLN) in 1993 set off a new round of guerrilla attacks and violence. The EZLN's members are young Mexicans disgusted with the poverty of the region. Nearly half of the households in the region where EZLN is based do not have running water, over 30 percent are *illiterate*, and another 30 percent do not have electricity in their homes. To make matters worse, the southern section of Mexico has long considered itself to be ignored in Mexico City, since the majority of economic development and infrastructure improvements have occurred in the north. A final problem that angered the EZLN was racism. The majority of these poor youth were of Mayan or other Indian descent, and they felt strongly that their rights should be given equal protection. In fact, many have compared the battles

The *Partido Revolucionario Nacional* was the dominant political party in Mexico from 1929 until the mid-seventies. President Callas originated the PNR with the intention of turning the basis of power in Mexico from the military and toward individual city-states. In reality, the party became so dominant in Mexico's political scene that no one outside the organization could hold office. The name of the organization changed after World War II, and became known as *Partido Revolucionario Institucional*, or the PRI.

55

fought by the EZLN to those fought by African Americans during the 1960s in the civil rights movement. Regardless of their intent, the EZLN used violence to seize control of several townships in 1993. To ease tension, the Mexican government agreed to build additional schools and roads in the area, as well as provide a source for fresh drinking water.

The environmental situation in Mexico also gives the government reason for concern. The many factories that provide jobs for the citizens of Mexico also cause air pollution, generating concern from the United States as well as other nations. Illegal logging and over-fishing the coastal areas are also major reasons for worry. Mexico has recently begun to monitor its environmental responsibilities more seriously, however; with the United States as a partner, it has established an intensive clean-up program.

The North American Trade Agreement (NAFTA) has helped the economy of Mexico to grow. This agreement was negotiated between Mexico, the United States, and Canada in the early 1990s, and it removes trade restrictions between these countries. The agreement provides opportunities for foreign companies to invest in Mexico. However, it is not the answer to all of Mexico's economic problems. In some instances, it has even created more problems. For instance, in 1995, more products were coming into the country than were going out, which hurt Mexico's economy. Also, American businesses who now do business in Mexico sometimes take advantage of the Mexican workers. The pay them very little and their factories often operate under unsafe conditions. However, foreign industries do provide more jobs, which helps boost the suffering economy.

While the problems that plague Mexico today are different from the ones faced by the natives who encountered the Spanish conquistadors, or the Spanish settlers who fought for their independence, today's dilemmas do have something in common with the ones faced by those long-ago people: the Mexican people have always been faced with differences in class, race, and religion. Hopefully with the reform that is occurring in the government, as well as the open trade that Mexico now enjoys with the United States and other countries, changes will occur. After its long and violent history, Mexico may finally have the peace and stability it needs to solve its many problems.

CHRONOLOGY

1000 B.C.	The Olmec civilization becomes a leader in development of writing, numbering, and astronomy.
400 B.C.	Olmec civilization disappears.
150 B.C.	Teotihuacán is built.
A.D. 750	Teotihuacán is abandoned.
300-900	Peak cultural growth of the Maya.
900-1200	Toltecs control much of Mexico.
1200	Aztecs begin to conquer other tribes for control of Mexico.
1325	Aztecs build Tenochtitlán.
1500	Aztecs control all land in central Mexico.
1517	Cordoba and Grijalva explore the coast of Mexico.
1519	Arrival of Cortés in Mexico.
1521	Spanish take control of Mexico.
1810	Grito de Delores calls for Mexico's independence from Spain.
1821	The Treaty of Cordoba grants Mexico its independence.
1833-1845	Santa Anna controls Mexico.
1836	Texas is granted independence from Spain in the Velasco Agreement.
1845	United States invites Texas to join the union, sparking the Mexican American War.
1854	Juárez becomes president of Mexico and implements a period of reform.
1862	France invades Mexico.

1876   Díaz begins his period of dictatorship.

1910   The Mexican Revolution begins.

1921   The end of the Revolution and the beginning of modern-day Mexico.

1938   President Cardenas nationalizes the petroleum industry and takes control of Mexico's oil reserves.

1962   Mexico pays off the debt that it incurred to buy back its petroleum reserves.

1968   Mexico hosts the Summer Olympic Games, and violence breaks out during a student protest.

1989   The first real opposition to the PRI, the conservative political party, is formed, the Partido de la Revolucion Democratica (PRD).

1993   The Zapatista National Liberation Army seizes control of several Mexican townships.

2000   Vicente Fox becomes the first president in over 70 years that is not a member of the PRI.

2001   President Fox meets with U.S. President George W. Bush to discuss a cooperative relationship between the neighboring countries.

2002   Latin American leaders, including Mexico's Vicente Fox, meet in Argentina for the Global Alumni Conference to discuss technological and economic issues.

GLOSSARY

Asset	An advantage or resource.
Armada	A fleet of Spanish warships.
Civil	Having to do with citizens; a civil war is fought between citizens of the same country.
Colonialism	Control of one power or nation over a dependent area or people.
Conquistadors	The Spanish conquerors of the New World.
Conservative	Wanting to maintain things the way they are with no reforms or changes; the opposite of liberal.
Constitution	The basic principles and laws of a country.
Coup	A violent overturn of the government.
Crossbows	A weapon made by setting a short bow crosswise at the end of a beam used to shoot square-headed bolts or arrows.
Democracy	The system of government where the people of the country elect their leaders to represent their interests.
Empire	A nation that is ruled by an emperor, a ruler with absolute power.
Exiled	Sent away from one's home or country.
Exports	Products or commodities that are shipped out of a country.
Guerilla	A warfare technique involving surprise attacks and sabotage.
Illiterate	Unable to read or write.
Infrastructure	A country's system of public works (such as roads, schools, railroads, etc.).
Liberal	Believing in progress and the protection of human rights; the opposite of conservative.

Peso	The Mexican unit of money.
Republic	A government where the chief of state is usually elected and does not have absolute power.
Rigged	Controlled by dishonest means.
Rigging	The lines and chains used on a ship to support and move the sails and masts.
Smallpox	A contagious disease that causes high fevers and pus-filled sores that leave deep scars.
Strikes	Refusals to work in an attempt to gain better working conditions or higher pay.
Succeeded	Followed; came next as an official or leader.

FURTHER READING

Fehrenbach, T. R. *Fire and Blood, a History of Mexico*. New York: Da Capo Press, 1995.

Goodwin, William. *Mexico: Modern Nations of the World*. San Diego: Lucent Press, 1999.

Kimmel, Eric A. *Montezuma and the Fall of the Aztecs*. New York: Holiday House, 2000.

Meyer, Michael C. *The Oxford History of Mexico*. New York: Oxford University Press, 2000.

Warburton, Lois. *World History Series—Aztec Civilization*. San Diego: Lucent Press, 1995.

Werner, Michael. *The History of Mexico: History, Culture, and Society*. Chicago: Fitzroy Dearborn Publishers, 1997.

INTERNET RESOURCES

The History of Mexico

http://www.go2mexico.com/article/history/
http://www.mexconnect.com/mex_/history/historyindex.html
http://lanic.utexas.edu/la/Mexico

The Government of Mexico

http://www.odci.gov/cia/publications/factbook/geos/mx.html
http://www.behindthelabel.org
http://www.mexicolaw.com

PICTURE CREDITS

2:	Corbis Images
10:	Giraudon/Art Resource, NY
13:	Danny Lehman/Corbis
14:	IMS Communications
16:	Charles and Josette Lenars/Corbis
18:	Hulton/Archive
21:	Firenze/Biblioteca Nazionale/Art Resource, NY
22:	Galleria degli Uffizi/Firenze/Art Resource, NY
25:	Charles and Josette Lenars/Corbis
26:	Dave G. Houser/Corbis
29:	Archivo Iconografico, S.A./Corbis
30:	Austrian Archives/Corbis
33:	Bettmann/Corbis
34:	Archivo Iconografico, S.A./Corbis
37:	Texas State Library and Archives Commission
38:	Hulton/Archive
41:	Corbis
42:	Hulton/Archive
45:	Corbis
46:	Hulton/Archive
49:	Corbis
50:	AFP/Corbis
52:	Bettmann/Corbis
53:	Hulton/Archive
54:	Reuters NewMedia Inc./Corbis

Cover: (front) Corbis Images
(inset) Reuters NewMedia Inc./Corbis
(back) Galleria degli Uffizi/Firenze/ Art Resource, NY

INDEX

Allende, Ignacio, 31–33
Aztec civilization, 16–17, 19–24

Bonaparte, Napoleon, 30, 40

Calles, Plutarco Elias, 46, 49
Cardenas, Lazaro, 49–51
Carranza, Venustiano, 46–47
Charles III, king of Spain, 28
Columbus, Christopher, 19
Cordoba, Francisco Hernandez de, 19
Cortés, Hernán, 19–24
Costilla, Miguel Hidalgo y, 31–33
Cuauhtemoc, 23, 24

Díaz, Porfirio, 41, 43–45
Doña Marina, 20

Gadsden Purchase, 37
Grivalva, Juan de, 19

Huastecs, 16
Huerta, Victoriano, 45–46

Juárez, Benito, 38, 40, 41, 43

Lerdo, Sebastian, 41
Limantour, Jose Ives, 43

Madero, Francisco, 44–45
Maximilian, archduke of Austria, 40–41
Mayan civilization, 15, 17, 25
Mixtees, 12, 16
Montezuma II, 19, 21

Nahuatl, 17

Napoleon III, 38–41
North American Free Trade Agreement
    (NAFTA), 56

Obregon, Alvaro, 46–47, 49
O'Donoju, Juan, 33
Olmec civilization, 11–12
Ordaz, Gustavo Díaz, 51
Orozco, Pascual, 45

Plan de Iguala, 33

Roosevelt, Franklin D., 51

Santa Anna, Antonio López de, 36–37
Spain, 19, 27, 28, 31, 33, 35, 38, 40
Spaniards, 17, 19–25, 28, 31, 36

Tarascans, 16
Taylor, Zachary, 36
Tenochtitlán, 17, 20, 21, 22, 23
Tepanecs, 17
Teotihuacán, 12, 15
Toltec civilization, 16, 17
Treaty of Cordoba, 33
Treaty of Guadalupe Hidalgo, 37

Velasco Agreement, 36
Velazquez, Diego, 19
Villa, Pancho, 45–46

Wilson, Woodrow, 46

Zapata, Emiliano, 45
Zapotecs, 12, 16
Zedillo, Ernesto, 53

CONTRIBUTORS

Roger E. Hernández is the most widely syndicated columnist writing on Hispanic issues in the United States. His weekly column, distributed by King Features, appears in some 40 newspapers across the country, including the *Washington Post, Los Angeles Daily News, Dallas Morning News, Arizona Republic, Rocky Mountain News* in Denver, *El Paso Times*, and *Hartford Courant*. He is also the author of *Cubans in America*, an illustrated history of the Cuban presence in what is now the United States, from the early colonists in 16th-century Florida to today's Castro-era exiles. The book was designed to accompany a PBS documentary of the same title.

Hernández's articles and essays have been published in the *New York Times, New Jersey Monthly, Reader's Digest*, and *Vista Magazine*; he is a frequent guest on television and radio political talk shows, and often travels the country to lecture on his topic of expertise. Currently, he is teaching journalism and English composition at the New Jersey Institute of Technology in Newark, where he holds the position of writer-in-residence. He is also a member of the adjunct faculty at Rutgers University.

Hernández left Cuba with his parents at the age of nine. After living in Spain for a year, the family settled in Union City, New Jersey, where Hernandez grew up. He attended Rutgers University, where he earned a BA in Journalism in 1977; after graduation, he worked in television news before moving to print journalism in 1983. He lives with his wife and two children in Upper Montclair, New Jersey.

Amy N. Hunter is a writer from Ripley, West Virginia. She writes most frequently on business and technical matters but enjoys working on young adult pieces as well.